Super Sitter's Playbook

games and activities for
a smart girl's guide: babysitting

by Aubre Andrus
illustrated by Karen Wolcott

Published by American Girl Publishing
Copyright © 2014 American Girl

Questions or comments? Call 1-800-845-0005,
visit **americangirl.com**, or write to Customer Service,
American Girl, 8400 Fairway Place, Middleton, WI 53562-0497.

Printed in China
14 15 16 17 18 19 20 21 LEO 10 9 8 7 6 5 4 3 2 1

All American Girl marks are trademarks of American Girl.

Editorial Development: Carrie Anton, Darcie Johnston
Art Direction & Design: Jessica Meihack
Production: Tami Kepler, Judith Lary, Paula Moon, Janell Wisecup, Jeannette Bailey
Special thanks to Ariel, Jamie, and Jessica

Dear Reader,

So, you're ready to be a babysitter? Congrats to you! Once you've taken the sitter safety classes, memorized the rules, asked the right questions, and read *A Smart Girl's Guide: Babysitting,* it will be time to let the good times roll with games, recipes, crafts, and more.

This book will help you keep the kids entertained from hello to good-bye—or good night. Thanks to the ideas here, the kids you sit for will have such a great time that they won't want you to leave. But watching children isn't just fun and games, so we've also included strategies for getting you through such dreaded babysitting scenarios as "I'm bored!" or "I don't want to!"

It doesn't matter how old the children are because many of the ideas in this book can be adjusted for any age. Make a craft more detailed for older kids. Or simplify a game to make it less tricky for little ones. Just use your best judgment, because all kids are unique. The end goal is to keep the children both busy and happy.

We know you have what it takes to be a confident and creative babysitter. This book should make your job easier. Good luck!

Your friends at American Girl

contents

sitter skills

Skills check! Find out how much know-how you've got when it comes to caring for kids and dealing with common babysitting challenges. For every question, circle all answers that apply to you.

1. When it comes to babysitting, I'm really good at ...
   ★ making funny voices when playing pretend.
   ★ turning frowns upside down and cheering an upset child.
   ★ putting the kids to bed.

2. For each babysitting job, I bring a ...
   ★ Super Sitter's Bag with books, craft supplies, and more.
   ★ snack for myself in case I don't like the food at the house.
   ★ mental list of games we can play together.

3. When the kids want to play, I ...
   - ★ join them in whatever activity they choose.
   - ★ help them come up with a few ideas.
   - ★ have so much fun—I feel like a little kid again!

4. At the kids' house, I know exactly where ...
   - ★ the craft supplies are.
   - ★ all the good snacks are.
   - ★ the bandages are, in case anyone gets hurt.

5. When it comes to these kids, I know ...
   - ★ whether or not they have allergies.
   - ★ their favorite pj's and bedtime routines.
   - ★ how to calm them down when their parents leave.

Count up all of the answers circled, and give yourself a point for each one.

Superstar Sitter

10 to 15 points: There's no babysitting challenge you can't handle. And the best part is that you enjoy it! You can play along with the kids when it's playtime, but you're not afraid to let them know you're in charge *all* the time. Keep up the great work!

Rising Name in Babysitting

5 to 9 points: The parents on the block know they can rely on you for kid care. You're building up your sitting skills and getting more experience all the time. With the tips and tricks in this book, you're soon to be a superstar.

Novice Nanny

4 points or less: You're on your way in the caregiving world. While you're not ready to watch the neighbor's twin toddlers on your own, you have what it takes to entertain your younger siblings or be a parent's helper to a family friend. With more experience— and by reading this book—you'll learn tips and tricks that can help make every babysitting job go smoothly.

getaway play-by-plays

Good-byes can be sad, especially for younger kids. Don't take it personally. It doesn't mean they are scared of you or don't like you. Some kids are just more attached to their parents. One of the first babysitting tasks is to help Mom and Dad get out the door with the least amount of distress possible. When the time comes, try these exit strategies to tone down tears and tantrums.

The Tour

Ask the child to give you a tour of the home. This is a great approach if it's the first time you're babysitting for this family or if they've recently moved to a new home or redecorated. Even if the parents have already shown you the basics—the location of the bathroom, where the emergency numbers are kept, where movies are stored—you can rely on the kids to show you the best toy in the house, the perfect place for a blanket fort, and where Mom and Dad keep the tastiest snacks.

Say: "I've never been here before. Can you show me around the house? I'd love to meet your favorite stuffed animals."

If you've babysat for the family before but haven't been there in a while, ask the child if anything has changed or if she has any new favorite books or games.

The Pet

If the family has a pet, suggest that you two attend to it (if it's OK with the parents, of course). Check on the hamster's wheel, take the dog out for a walk, or feed the fish. It will take the child's mind off the long good-bye and focus it on a specific task.

Say: "Hey, how's Noodles doing? Let's go say hi and see if he needs a treat."

The Surprise

Bring over a game, toy, book, or movie the child can borrow for the night. Keep it tucked away when you first arrive, and wait to take it out until just before the parents leave. Make it a big deal, emphasizing how special it is and describing all the details while Mom and Dad head out the door.

Say: "While your parents are getting ready, I have to show you this cool pop-up book I brought. I think you're going to love it. It has more than 50 different animals! Let's see if we can count them all."

The Activity

Kids love when you ask their opinions and when they can help you make decisions. Bring over an easy craft project such as a friendship bracelet or a drawing (one that you don't mind sharing), and ask the kids if they can help you finish.

Say: "I'm working on this friendship bracelet. I'm stuck on what colors I should use next. Do you think you can help me pick one and then finish making it?"

The Snack

If the timing makes sense, suggest that you and the child head to the kitchen to start making a snack or a meal. Need a recipe idea that doesn't require any adult supervision? Turn to page 30 for some great ideas.

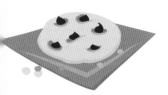

Say: "I'm really hungry! What about you? Will you help me make a new recipe? I need a taste tester."

Safe Snacks

👋 Never feed kids without talking to the parents first. Find out if they're allergic to anything or not allowed to eat certain kinds of foods because of their culture, religion, or family rules.

kid q&a

The better you and the kids get to know one another, the more fun you'll have—and the easier your job will be. Ask them the following questions, and write down their answers on a separate sheet of paper. They will feel important knowing that you're keeping track of their likes and dislikes. And you can save the info for the next time you sit for them.

Kid Questionnaire

First name: Age:

....

What's your favorite color?

....

What's your favorite movie, book, or TV show?

....

What's your favorite subject in school?

....

What's your favorite sport?

....

What do you want to be when you grow up?

....

If you could go anywhere in the world, where would it be?

....

What's the most fun day you've ever had?

....

What's your favorite thing to do?

....

would you rather?

make a craft **OR**
play a game?

read a book **OR**
watch a movie?

play inside **OR**
play outside?

do a jigsaw puzzle **OR**
solve a word puzzle?

play a board game **OR**
play an active game?

draw a picture **OR**
write a story?

Tots' Turn

Make a Sitter version of this Kid Questionnaire, and bring a copy in your Super Sitter's Bag. Give it to the kids and let them interview you. If they're too young to read and write, just set a timer for 3 minutes and tell them it's their turn to ask you about your interests.

kid categories

Like snowflakes, no two kids are alike. Each has a distinct and unique personality—just like you and your friends. Become a better babysitter by understanding and adjusting to each child's feelings, insecurities, and likes and dislikes.

Seriously Shy Shayla

Body Language: She makes little eye contact, doesn't talk much, keeps her head down, and tends to hide or peek around corners.
Pros: If she doesn't come out of her shell, you're almost guaranteed a quiet, drama-free sitting session.
Cons: It may be hard to entertain and feed her since you won't know her likes and dislikes.
Warning: You might think she doesn't like you.
Don't: Overwhelm her. She needs time to warm up to new people.
Do: Introduce yourself. Make the transition from stranger to friend by sharing interesting facts about yourself. You could even talk about the fun things you do with other kids for whom you babysit.

When the timing is right, try asking her some questions, too.

Say: "When I'm not babysitting, I take art classes. Do you want me to show you how to draw a cat? I'm really good at it. What's your favorite thing to draw?"

High-Energy Hannah

Body Language: This girl runs around the house or jumps on the couches—anything but sitting still.
Pros: High-energy kids typically love to play games, which can help to wear them

out and get them ready for some downtime, such as watching a movie.
Cons: She might have a hard time listening when she's so excited.
Warning: You need to establish that you're in charge while the parents are gone. Otherwise she may not listen to you at all.
Don't: Yell. Instead, be friendly but firm.
Do: Introduce her to a safe, active game that will keep the energy level high but in control. Turn to page 19 for ideas.

Say: "Jumping on the couch isn't safe. If you stop now and sit down by me, I'll teach you a really fun game."

Can't-Stop-Crying Carrie

Body Language: She gets easily agitated by brothers or sisters, and crosses her arms and pouts if she doesn't get her way.
Pros: Activity selection will be easy. You'll quickly see that something low-conflict such as a craft or coloring sheet will be a better choice than playing games.
Cons: Constant crying can be frustrating for siblings who may not want to play with her, and it can wear on your nerves.
Warning: Sometimes the crying is fake and just a call for attention.
Don't: Force her to do anything. She probably won't be ready to jump back into the fun until she's calmed down.
Do: Acknowledge her frustration, then ease her slowly into a solo activity such as reading a book or working on an activity sheet.

Say: "When I'm upset, I like to take my mind off it by reading a book. Let's take a little break with your favorite."

Won't-Listen Laurie

Body Language: She stays focused on having fun instead of hearing you out, and she doesn't make eye contact.

Pros: This girl is probably perfectly content entertaining herself.

Cons: She doesn't want to do the un-fun stuff, such as cleaning up or getting ready for bed.

Warning: Not listening can be frustrating, but you have to approach it with a thoughtful strategy.

Don't: Get upset. It will only make it worse.

Do: Offer a bit of help, but make sure she's doing most of the work. If she doesn't want to clean up, tell her you'll help with one task while she works on another.

Say: "I know you don't want to clean up, so I'll give you some help. How about I clean up the dishes while you put away your toys?"

Just-a-Toddler Tanya

Body Language: This little one can walk around but sometimes falls. She's interested in touching everything.

Pros: Toddlers can be adorable! And you can keep them entertained with the simplest activities.

Cons: Toddlers need your attention at all times.

Warning: Before the parents leave, ask them to point out any dangerous areas of the house, such as an easily opened door that leads to a stairwell. Also ask if there are any off-limits locations.

Don't: Leave the child alone—ever. If you have to use the bathroom, make sure she's safely secured in a playpen or crib.

Do: Pick up the child if she cries, and calm her by rubbing her back.

Say: Almost anything! Just keep talking to toddlers to let them know you're attentive.

make an entrance

Take this quiz to see if you should start off the night with a cute craft, an exciting game, or a yummy treat.

1. How many times have you babysat this family?
   a. I've been here a few times.
   b. We see each other a lot. This is the family I know best.
   c. I've babysat them only once before.

2. What are the kids like when you arrive?
   a. They're really energized.
   b. They seem kind of bored.
   c. They seem a little sad that their parents are leaving.

3. To the best of your knowledge, how would you describe these kids?
   a. Sometimes they don't listen because they're busy running around.
   b. They're creative and like to play.
   c. They're good listeners.

4. At this house, which of the following is most true?

   a. There is a lot of room to play inside and outside.

   b. I know my way around the big kitchen.

   c. The playroom is filled with cool craft supplies.

5. What happened the last time you babysat these kids?

   a. The neighbor children came over to play in the backyard.

   b. They played and didn't need me to take the lead.

   c. I had trouble keeping them entertained.

Answers

If you picked **more a's,** these kids want action. See page 19 for some great game ideas that will keep them active and entertained both indoors and out.

If you picked **more b's,** tummies are rumbling and a snack is in order. Turn to page 30 for treats and eats.

If you picked **more c's,** or if you've never babysat these kids, creative juices are flowing. Turn to page 23 for craft ideas that both boys and girls will love.

go-to games

FINISH

START

Every babysitter needs a few games in her arsenal, and we've listed some great ones here. These boredom-busting, kid-approved activities have been popular for decades. You can modify them for any age group and almost any situation. Game on!

Scavenger Hunt

For a happy hunt, you'll need a goal—a hidden prize, the answer to a riddle, or a fun activity at the end. Lead the kids to the finish line by drawing a map and leaving hidden objects or clues at each spot marked along the way. Here are two examples:

★ Place one letter of the alphabet (written on a piece of scrap paper) at each stop along the map. Once the kids have collected all the letters, they can unscramble them to spell out the name of that night's dinner or even the location of a hidden prize.

★ Draw a map that leads kids to stuffed animals that you've hidden around the house. By the end, the kids will have collected a whole zoo to play with!

Obstacle Course

Create courses that you can modify for different ability levels and ages. If you're watching more than one child, make multiple courses according to their ages, or let the younger kids skip an obstacle. Try these ideas:

★ With a parent's permission in advance, draw a path with chalk on the driveway. Place a jump rope, a Hula hoop, and a basketball evenly along the route. At each station, kids have to perform the action (jumping, twirling, or dribbling) 10 times before moving on to the next.

★ Set up a drawing obstacle course around a kitchen table. Leave paper, pencils, and a random object such as a stuffed animal or a piece of fruit at each station. Kids must sketch each object as fast as they can before moving on to the next one. At the end, take a look at all the speedy doodles and have a good laugh!

Hide-and-Seek

There are lots of variations on this classic game, and the simplest is peekaboo. Babies love when you cover your face for a couple seconds and then pop out with a surprised "Peekaboo!" Even toddlers get a kick out of this game. Here are a few variations for older kids:

★ Tell the hiders to hide stuffed animals throughout the house. The seeker must find all the missing animals. The hiders can give clues by making animal noises whenever the seeker is getting close.

★ In this variation called Sardines, one person hides while everyone else counts. When a seeker discovers the hider, the seeker hides with her. When the next seeker finds them, she hides with them, too, and so on until the last seeker finds the whole group.

Follow the Leader

This is a great go-to game for when you need the kids to listen. Be the leader when you're ready to head inside after playing in the backyard, making sure to zig and zag, skip and hop, and logroll your way to the door to make it interesting. Here are two more ideas:

★ Try a game of Follow the Leader—on paper. The kids have to copy exactly what you draw, one step at a time. You draw a shape, then the child next to you follows, and then the child next to her follows.

★ Combine Simon Says and Follow the Leader. The kids can't repeat your action unless you say "Simon says" before naming the action. Try this game before bedtime, and sneak in "Simon says brush your teeth" and "Simon says put on your pajamas."

Don't be just a bystander. Get in the game and play along!

Instant Fun

Bring these items along on your next babysitting adventure, and you'll always be ready when the kids say, "I'm bored!"

- ★ **Chalk:** Play school, trace each other's bodies on the driveway and draw clothes on the outlines, or create a gigantic maze that kids can walk through.

- ★ **Bubbles:** Conduct a bubble-popping or biggest-bubble contest, or see if anyone can catch a bubble without popping it.

- ★ **Playing Cards:** Try to build a card house or castle, or play classic games such as Memory or Go Fish.

Let's Pretend

Kids have wild imaginations, so put them to good use. They will love it if you really get into the game and act your heart out. Don't be embarrassed to give it your all. Give these pretending games a go:

- ★ Do a role reversal. Have the kids pretend to be the baby-sitter and you pretend to be the kid. Or pretend the kids are animals and you're a pet sitter—kids love to act silly.

- ★ Make up a story line for the whole night. Change your names and imagine you live in a faraway place. Let the kids help you create the story.

- ★ Create characters with hats and other distinctive dress-up items that you find or bring with you. Make up funny skits together.

kid-winning crafts

A portable craft kit might be a good investment. Include supplies like kid-safe scissors, colored paper, glue sticks, and crayons.

Kids love to show off their crafty creations when Mom and Dad come home. Bring the necessary supplies, be ready to assist the kids throughout the process, and encourage them with kind words if they get frustrated. On the following pages you'll find a few crafts that kids of all ages will love to do together or on their own.

Ages 3–6
Toy Town

Gather sheets of construction paper, shoe boxes, and more to create a town that stretches throughout the house.

Build It: Start with a winding Main Street of paper, and add streets to it. Together, decorate the boxes to look like buildings, using your own town or famous cities as inspiration. Make each piece as detailed as you like so that you'll have just as much fun creating the town as you do playing in it.

Play in It: You have an entire make-believe town in which to play. If rolling cars up and down the street gets boring, give these ideas a try:

★ Transport stuffed animals from one side of town to the other with cars and trucks.

★ If your streets make up a flat-enough surface, challenge each other to a car race.

★ Turn a piece of paper into a parking lot, or glue toilet paper tubes in a pyramid to create a parking garage for toy cars. And don't forget to add action figures as people!

Pack & Play Town

Use strips of gray fabric or felt to make a portable "street" that you take with you to different babysitting jobs. Create roads that turn, adding yellow lines with dimensional fabric paint and traffic signs made from cardboard, construction paper, and craft sticks.

Bubble Art

This craft is for outdoors only! You'll need a bottle of bubbles, three plastic cups, three colors of food coloring, and white paper. Pour a small amount of bubbles into each cup. Add one drop of food coloring to each. Lay paper on grass, and challenge kids to aim their bubbles so they land on each piece. When the bubbles land and pop, they'll turn the paper into a colorful work of art. Let dry before bringing inside. Warning: Food coloring can stain, so cover the kids in old shirts or smocks.

Turn to the back of the book to find these garland templates:

★ hearts
★ outer space
★ garden
★ kites

Great Garland

For this cute décor craft, make reusable templates by tracing the shapes in the back of the book onto heavy paper and cutting them out. Along with your templates, you'll need ribbon, tape, scissors, colored paper, and decorating supplies such as crayons and stickers.

1. Using the templates you made, trace the shape or shapes of choice onto sheets of decorative or construction paper. Cut them out. For a longer garland, trace and cut out more shapes.

2. Tape the shapes together to form flowers, planets with moons or rings, and kites with tails. Decorate them.

3. Line up the items on the floor with a little space between them. Lay a piece of ribbon that's longer than the lineup on top.

4. Attach the ribbon to each item with a small piece of tape.

Garland Safety

✋ Garland should be hung in a family area, never in a kid's room. Have the parents hang the garland in a safe location, and never let a child play with the garland or the ribbon.

Monster Chest

Turn an empty tissue box of any size or shape into a monster! The opening of the box is the mouth—cut two strips of pointy teeth from colored felt and attach them to the edges of the box opening with tape or adhesive dots. Cut paper half circles for eyes, and attach them to the top edge of the box. Finish by adding stickers, yarn hair, or whatever else the kids can dream up! Optional: First trace each side of the box onto felt. Cut out felt pieces and attach to the box with glue to create a furry base.

Art for All

Every kid has a different ability level when it comes to art. Be ready to assist with cutting and drawing, and don't be afraid to alter the directions to make them easier for a child who's struggling with a craft.

Use it as a monster mailbox or as a place to store secret collections.

Ages 7–9
Secret Wish Book

Turn a small jewelry box into a secret book of wishes and dreams. Kids can draw their dream pet, dream playhouse, dream name—any wish!—on the pages. Younger kids can use stickers.

1. Cut two long, narrow strips from a sheet of 8½-by-11-inch paper. Each strip should be 11 inches long, and the width should be less than the bottom of the box.

2. Glue the two strips end to end, so that the final length is more than 20 inches.

3. Accordion-fold the long paper strip so that it fits neatly inside the box.

4. Unfold the paper. Draw a picture on each "page" made by the folds, both front and back.

5. With a glue stick, glue one end of the paper strip to the inside bottom of the box. Glue the other end to the inside of the lid.

6. Place the lid on the box to make the wish book secret!

Tiny Bed

Transform a small, rectangular cardboard box (found at craft stores) into toy furniture.

1. Cut a strip of felt the same width as the bottom of the box and about 2 inches longer.

2. Glue the felt to the bottom of the box. Then fold over the extra length of felt to make a pillow, as shown. Secure it at the edge with glue.

3. Cut a blanket the same width as the box, but a little shorter in length. This will go over the figurine to tuck it into bed.

4. To make a headboard, cut a piece of felt that fits in the box top and glue it in place. Finish by decorating the bed and blanket with felt or dimensional fabric paint.

Creative Constructions

This bed is a perfect size for tiny figurines or stuffed animals. Use a bigger box for a bigger toy. Or try turning different-sized boxes into other pieces of furniture, such as a nightstand or a dresser, for an entire collection. If a craft is too easy for a kid, encourage her to put her own personal touch on it by using an additional craft supply that's not mentioned in the directions. Or ask kids to make another project for their parents—or you!—or to help their younger sibling.

snacks that score

Always ask parents if a child has any allergies. Some kids are allergic to peanuts or dairy products, so don't serve these foods until you know they're safe.

When it comes to babysitting, sandwiches and snack mixes are your best friends. Use the ideas on the following pages to turn making and eating treats into a fun activity. If you're preparing food without little helpers, be sure to keep them in the kitchen with you, under your watchful eye.

Snack Smorgasbord

Set out a buffet and let the kids create their own cuisines.

★ Use a butter knife to cut a turkey and cheese sandwich and a peanut butter and jelly sandwich diagonally into four triangular pieces each. Set out the sandwich triangles, and let the kids mix and match them on a small plate.

★ Fill five small bowls with the following ingredients: popcorn, pretzels, bite-sized cookies, cereal, and chocolate candies. Let kids fill up their own treat bowls with favorite combinations.

★ Pretend the kids are pirates or futuristic robots. Make a snack mix called Fish and Chips (fish-shaped crackers and potato chips) or Nuts and Bolts (pretzel sticks and different-shaped cereals).

Sushi Sandwich Rolls

A fish-free version of sushi is sure to please! For extra fun, try to eat the rolls with chopsticks.

1. Flatten a slice of bread by placing a napkin over it and pressing down softly with your palm. Cut off the crusts.

2. Make one of these rolls or create your own:

   ★ Spread mayonnaise or mustard onto the flattened bread. Add a slice of turkey. Place a string cheese stick at one edge.

   ★ Spread on a thin layer of peanut butter, then top with jelly.

   ★ Spread on cream cheese. Place bits of celery and carrot at one edge.

3. Roll up the bread and ingredients, starting with the edge that has the most ingredients. With a clean butter knife, cut each roll into three or four pieces.

Edible Art

Show kids how to turn an afternoon snack into a work of delicious animal art.

★ **Banana Butterfly:** Cut off the ends of a peeled banana. Make vertical slits at the sides and insert pretzel wings. Add chocolate chip eyes and pretzel stick antennae.

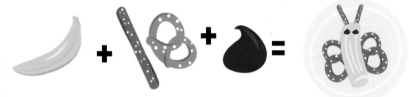

★ **Owl-wich:** Any sandwich can transform into an owl with diagonal slices for wings, cucumber slice eyes with raisins on top, and a cheese triangle beak.

★ **Teddy Bear Toast:** Spread peanut butter on toast. Add halved banana slices for ears and raisins for eyes. Stack a banana slice with a raisin on top for a nose.

Dainty Desserts

It's nearly impossible to get through a babysitting session without the kids asking for cookies or candy. As long as the parents said it's OK, try these recipes to satisfy a child's sweet tooth.

★ **Funny Yummy:** Decorate a small, clear plastic cup with googly eyes and a marker face. Fill it with colored yogurt and top with sprinkles and a spoon.

★ **S'more on a Stick:** Insert a pretzel stick into a marshmallow. Dip the marshmallow into a small bowl filled with chocolate syrup, then roll it in a small bowl filled with crushed graham crackers.

TIP: Crush the graham crackers by placing a couple of crackers in a sealed sandwich bag. Tap lightly with a spoon.

★ **PB Bites:** Scoop peanut butter onto a spoon and top it with chocolate chips or sprinkles.

Your Order, Please?

Pretend you're a waitress and the kids are customers at a restaurant. Seat the kids at a table with place settings (minus the knives) and a menu with two or three options. Take their food and drink order, then serve them. You can even give them pretend money to pay. If the kids are older, do the reverse and let them serve you.

super sitter strategies

You're in charge. You want to be friends with the kids, but sometimes you have to act more like a parent or teacher. If they need to finish homework or do chores, it's your job to make sure it gets done. If a clean house turns into a big mess, it's your responsibility to get the kids to help pick up before the parents come home. And when things just don't go as expected, it's up to you to make a new game plan.

when good plans go bad

Even the most prepared babysitter can't plan for everything. When a thunderstorm ruins outside activities or when the kids are just tired and crabby, it's up to you to find a way through the challenge!

Stormy Weather?

Watching a favorite movie is an easy rainy day fix, but it's not a perfect replacement for the energy the kids could've burned off in the backyard. Instead, clear a bit of space near the TV, and pair up an exercise activity with something specific happening in the movie. For example, during a wizard movie, have everyone do 10 jumping jacks each time a spell is cast. For a pirate movie, have everyone run in place for the entire length of time a parrot talks.

> Select a movie that the kids have watched over and over again so that they can help assign the exercises.

Overdue Adults?

Even if the kids have had a great time, some of them may be counting down the minutes until their parents return. If you get a call

that the parents are running late, redirect the kids' attention toward an activity that involves their parent in some way. Say, *"Your mom will be here in 20 minutes. That's just enough time to make a drawing for her. She'll be so excited to see your hard work!"*

Bored or Boo-hoos?

You babysit this family all the time, and the kids are not getting excited about any of your ideas. Or maybe two siblings just fought with each other and now everyone's upset. You know you need to change the mood, but you're just not sure what to do. Here's a secret: You don't need a new idea—you just need to present the idea in a new way.

* **Do Something New:** Scatter the What Now? cards (from the back of this book) around the house, and let the kids discover a new activity in each room.

* **Change the Location:** Play a board game in the backyard, or eat a snack inside an indoor blanket tent.

* **Add a Twist:** Get creative and change one rule or step in a normal activity. Try drawing with your eyes closed or eating opposite-handed.

Quiz

up for the challenge?

Watching kids and being in an unfamiliar home can bring on a few common babysitting fears. Take this quiz to find out which one you're most concerned about—and how to handle it.

1. When a kid cries, I worry that . . .
   a. she won't stop crying. Ever.
   b. she'll tell her parents that I was mean.
   c. something is seriously wrong with her.

2. When I meet a family for the first time, I . . .
   a. talk about all the fun things I'll do with the kids.
   b. get really nervous.
   c. ask a lot of questions about allergies and safety.

3. My least favorite part about babysitting is . . .
   a. making the kids clean up when they don't want to.
   b. wondering what the kids will tell their parents.
   c. when a kid falls and gets a scraped knee.

4. Sometimes I spend a lot of time . . .

   a. planning games and activities—we never have time for them all.

   b. worrying about what I'll say to the parents when they come home.

   c. asking the parents questions before they leave.

5. I bring a _____ with me to every babysitting job.

   a. little toy or present

   b. list of references

   c. first-aid kit

6. The thing I say most when babysitting is . . .

   a. "What do you want to do next?"

   b. "I don't think your parents will like that."

   c. "Be careful!"

Answers

If you picked **more a's,** you're afraid the kids won't have fun.

Babysitting is a balance between having fun and making sure kids follow the rules. Put your foot down when you need to. Safety is most important. And remember that you don't have to bring a new craft or game idea every time, but you should take part in whatever fun the kids are having. If you are friendly and try your best, you and the kids will get along great.

If you picked **more b's,** you're afraid the family won't like you.

Talking to adults can be scary, especially when they are paying you for your work. The parents might not praise your work every time—after all, they weren't there to see it!—but you know whether or not you did a great job. If you keep the kids safe and happy, you'll be a superstar sitter. The more you babysit for a family, the more comfortable and confident you'll become.

If you picked **more c's,** you're afraid of an emergency.

As the babysitter, you're in charge of the kids' safety. And you know that safety trumps fun any day. You've already memorized the location of the first-aid kit and the list of emergency numbers. It's OK that you're overly cautious, but don't overreact in front of the kids. If something bad happens, keep calm. Kids sometimes get bumps and bruises. They'll cry, but then they'll get over it, and they'll be back to having fun before you know it. It's all part of being a kid.

top tips

Game Over

When it comes to cleanup, challenge the kids to clean as much as they can in 1 minute. (Make sure you play, too!) Declare a winner for each round based on the number of toys that players put away. Or assign each kid to a room (or a corner of a room), and see who can make the most mess go away in 3 minutes.

Say: "I'm challenging you to a cleaning contest. Do you think you can beat me? Here's how we'll keep score."

Break It Up

If you divide the tasks into smaller bits, they will seem more manageable. Tell the kids that they can have a short break if they work for 15 minutes straight. Then schedule another 15-minute work session soon after that.

Say: "You have to get this homework done before your parents get home. How about we work for 15 minutes, and then we'll take a 5-minute break so that we can practice a card trick together?"

Win-Win

If the kids want to give up midway, give them a prize to look forward to. If they complete all of their chores or homework, reward them with a cool craft, a delicious snack, or a fun game.

Say: "You're almost done. If you just finish these last five problems, then we can go outside and play on the swing set."

Stand firm. You don't always have to be the fun sitter who lets the kids do whatever they want. You're here to entertain, but the parents' rules and expectations come first.

bedtime tricks

The parents are staying out late, and they've asked you to put the kids to bed. Many kids have a specific bedtime routine—and if their parents aren't there to help them through it, they might act up. That's where the following tricks come in. Operation Bedtime can be a success if you come prepared.

Do a Dance

If a kid doesn't want to brush her teeth, ask if she's heard of the "Toothpaste Dance." Tell her you'll show it to her once she starts brushing. Now be prepared to get silly! As she's brushing, make up a dance (that still lets her brush!) such as looking to the left, then the right, then bending knees, then standing on toes. Keep going until she's done brushing. You can make up a dance that involves pajamas, getting into bed, or shutting off the lights, too.

Surefire Snooze Kit

Pack along a nightlight that plugs into any outlet, an extra stuffed animal, and a favorite bedtime story from when you were little. Explain to the kids that this is how you used to fall asleep and that you want to share the tradition with them.

Monster Mash

Nighttime fears—monsters, storms, and the dark—can be worse when parents are away. If a kid is scared, don't rush bedtime. Stay in his room for awhile. Read relaxing stories and sing soothing songs together. When you leave the room, keep a light on nearby and tell him you'll peek in every 10 minutes. (Then do it.)

great good-byes

The kids are in bed and you've got 30 minutes to yourself. Instead of turning on the TV—remember, you're still on the job!—do a sweep of the house. Clean up any messes made during your stay, and tidy up the family room. If there's still time, go above and beyond the call of duty with one of these end-of-the-night activities.

Sitter Summary

Give the parents a recap of the night in written form (see a sample in the back of the book). On a piece of notebook paper, create a bulleted list of the great things that happened while you babysat, including the activities you did, the games you played, and anything

cute or funny the kids said or did. If anything bad happened—for example, if the child misbehaved or got a paper cut—tell the parents before you leave.

Before the kids go to bed, ask them to help you draft this letter to their parents. They can sign it as well and leave a little note such as, "Can't wait to see you in the morning!"

Babysitting Badges

Create a simple award for the kids. Fold a strip of wide ribbon and attach it to the back of a paper circle with glue. The award can be a generic "#1 Kid" or something more specific, such as "Super Sharer Award" or "Great Gamer Award." Give the awards to the parents to pass on to their kids the next day.

Thank You

If it's your first time sitting for the family, leave behind a handmade card thanking them for hiring you. Include your phone number at the end, and remind them that you'd love to babysit again. Here's a sample: "Thanks so much for letting me watch Liam tonight. We had a ton of fun playing board games and making a snack. If you ever need a babysitter again, please give me a call at 555-1002! I'd love to help out again."

Art Show

If the kids made any crafts or drew pictures, be sure to show the artwork off to the parents before you leave. They'll be happy to see that you kept the kids entertained in a creative way.

extra points

Before heading off to a babysitting job, get some fun activities ready and have what you need to keep track of important info. Check out the games, crafts, and checklists on the next pages. Then visit **americangirl.com/play** and find even more to download and print for your Super Sitter's Bag.

What Now? Cards

Tear out these cards, cut them apart, and keep them in a large envelope in your sitter's bag. When the kids are feeling bored or if you're out of ideas, let the kids pick one randomly from the envelope. Also, feel free to expand on these cards by writing in your own ideas on the blank cards provided.

Great Garlands

These templates can be used over and over again. Make the templates and bring them, along with colored paper, ribbon, tape, and decorating supplies. (See page 26 for step-by-step instructions.)

Helpful Stuff

play A parent checklist, "Welcome Home!" sheet, and "Notes for Next Time" can be used every time you sit. Copy them from the book, or print them out at **americangirl.com/play**.

what?
now?

what?
now?

what?
now?

what?
now?

what?
now?

what?
now?

Great Game
Musical Chairs!
Play this game with toys. When the music stops, everyone plays with whatever toy is in front of them!

Great Game
Freeze Dance!
When the music plays, everyone has to dance like crazy. When the music stops, everyone has to freeze and hold their pose until the music starts again.

Great Game
Color Hunt!
Each player is given a bucket and told a color. On "go," players have to see how many toys and objects in their color they can collect in their buckets in 2 minutes.

Great Game
Stack It!
Use a stopwatch to see how quickly each player can stack and unstack plastic cups. Start with a 4-3-2-1 formation, and then keep adding on.

Great Game
Animal Charades!
Write the names of animals on cards. One person draws a card and acts like the animal— without making noises! The others guess the animal.

Great Game
You decide!

what?
now?

what?
now?

what?
now?

what?
now?

what?
now?

what?
now?

Role Reversal

Have a backward night. Say "hello!" when the parents leave, put on pajamas right away, then have dessert before dinner. Say "thank you" instead of "please" and "no" instead of "yes."

Role Reversal

Let the kids cook for you. Give them the supplies they need to make a snack mix or build a sandwich, and let them create something especially for you.

Role Reversal

Change your names for the day and call each other only by those names.

Role Reversal

Let the kids teach you how to play their favorite game or activity. Then teach them your favorite game or activity from when you were a kid.

Role Reversal

Turn a pair of old socks (ask your parents before bringing your own) into puppets by gluing felt pieces to create a face for each. Talk to each other using only the sock puppets.

Role Reversal

You decide!